TABLE OF CONTENTS

-CHAPTER ONE-
Columbus, Admiral of the Ocean Sea 4

-CHAPTER TWO-
Ponce de Leon, Explorer of Florida 12

-CHAPTER THREE-
Cartier Goes to Canada 18

-CHAPTER FOUR-
Coronado's Quest for Gold 22

-CHAPTER FIVE-
Drake Circles the World 28

-CHAPTER SIX-
Hudson Reaches New York 34

-CHAPTER SEVEN-
Joliet and Marquette Go Down the Mississippi 40

GLOSSARY 46
READ MORE 47
CRITICAL THINKING
USING THE COMMON CORE 47
INTERNET SITES 47
INDEX 48

-CHAPTER ONE-

Columbus, Admiral of the Ocean Sea

Three small wooden ships sailed out of the harbor of Palos, Spain, on August 3, 1492. Commanding this tiny fleet was Christopher Columbus. He was seeking a new route to southern Asia from Europe.

In those days many ships sailed south, around Africa, and then turned east. Columbus believed he could find a shorter route by sailing west. He had persuaded several wealthy Spaniards to pay for his voyage. Columbus also won the backing of King Ferdinand and Queen Isabella of Spain. Columbus would claim any lands he found for them. In return Ferdinand and Isabella promised to let him rule those lands for Spain. He could also earn money from the resources he found. And Columbus would receive the title "Admiral of the Ocean Sea."

After a little less than two months at sea, Columbus and his men reached land. But they had not reached Asia. Instead, they found islands in the Caribbean Sea. Soon Europeans would call those lands and the nearby continents "the New World." But they were hardly new to the people who had lived there for thousands of years. Still, Columbus's discovery changed history. It led to a permanent connection between the "Old World" of Europe and lands soon called the Americas.

Columbus leaves Spain thinking he is heading for India in 1492.

WHO WAS COLUMBUS?

Christopher Columbus's voyage made him one of the most famous figures in world history. But many mysteries swirl around the details of his life. By most accounts, he was born in 1451 in Genoa, Italy. Yet other sites claim to be his birthplace, and Columbus did not speak Italian. He was raised a Roman Catholic, but some scholars think his family had Jewish roots. During Columbus's lifetime, Spain forced Jews out of the country if they would not **convert** to the Catholic faith. Some Jews converted to Catholicism. Others pretended to become Catholic so they could remain in Spain. Columbus may have been one of those who pretended so he could stay in Spain.

What does seem true is that by the 1470s Columbus was a sailor on Portuguese ships that traveled to many European ports. He survived a shipwreck in 1476 and then sailed on voyages as far as West Africa. Portugal and other European nations wanted to trade in Africa and Asia. The desire for foreign riches set off what has been called the Age of Exploration. Columbus's voyage was part of that rush for wealth and control of foreign lands.

convert—to change religion

Christopher Columbus

TRIUMPH AND FAILURE

On the 1492 voyage to the west, Columbus and his crew of about 90 sailed on three ships: the *Nina*, the *Pinta*, and the *Santa Maria*. The sailors had to trust that Columbus was right—that they could cross the vast Atlantic Ocean and reach land. But as the trip dragged on, some of the men grumbled. They feared they would be lost at sea. Finally, on October 12, the ships reached one of the islands in the Bahamas, though which one is not known for sure. Columbus visited several islands in the area. He traded goods with the local people and ate local foods. Columbus called the land the "most … goodly that there is in the world."

Columbus sees the New World for the first time.

Columbus returned to Spain early in 1493 and was treated as a hero. Along with gold and other items, he returned with several American Indians he had captured. He already imagined using the local peoples of the New World as slaves. Columbus thought he had reached a part of Asia called the Indies, so he called the people Indians.

- DISCOVERY FACT -

Christopher Columbus believed that Solomon, a king in the Bible, had found huge gold mines in Asia. Columbus hoped to find those mines during his later voyages.

Columbus's routes to and from the New World

Columbus sailed to the New World three more times. Spain wanted to set up colonies in the lands it claimed and to convert the American Indians to Christianity. Columbus reached what is now Central America and South America and served as governor of Hispaniola, an island in the Caribbean Sea east of Cuba. Columbus did not find all the riches he sought. He returned to Spain for the last time in 1504 and died in 1506.

For Spain, Columbus's voyages led to the creation of an empire in the New World. Columbus's arrival also led to the Taino and Arawak Indians of the Caribbean and many other American Indians being enslaved by Europeans or killed by diseases brought from Europe. Because of this, some people today do not consider Columbus a hero, as many Americans with European roots once did. Still, no one disputes that his explorations made—and changed—history.

THE COLUMBIAN EXCHANGE

Columbus's voyages led to what is sometimes called the Columbian Exchange. Crops and goods from Europe, Asia, and Africa ended up in the Americas for the first time. Meanwhile, the Spaniards brought some of the goods they found to Europe and later took them to Asia and Africa.

Some products that came from the Americas included tomatoes, potatoes, corn, and hot chili peppers. The Spaniards brought the first horses, cattle, and pigs to the New World. They also had guns, which the American Indians didn't have. Better weapons helped the Europeans when they battled American Indians who tried to resist their rule.

-CHAPTER TWO-

Ponce de Leon, Explorer of Florida

One of the sailors who may have traveled with Christopher Columbus on his second voyage to the New World was Juan Ponce de Leon. He was born in 1460 in the Spanish town of Santervás de Campos. During that time, Spain, which was a Christian country, was often at war with the Moors, who were Muslim. The Moors traced their roots to North Africa and had captured Spain centuries before. Ponce de Leon probably took part in battles that drove the Moors out of the country.

If he did sail with Columbus, de Leon was one of about 1,200 men sent to start a Spanish colony on the island of Hispaniola. Hispaniola is now known as Haiti and the Dominican Republic. The members of the **expedition** also discovered other islands in the Caribbean Sea. De Leon was thought to be in the region again in 1502, serving as a captain in the Spanish army. He helped defeat Carib Indians who were rebelling against Spanish rule. As a reward, de Leon was made governor of part of Hispaniola.

expedition—a journey made for a particular reason

Ponce de Leon

Ponce de Leon encounters American Indians in Florida.

THE SEARCH FOR GOLD

Like other Spanish **conquistadors**, de Leon wanted to find gold in the New World. When he heard there might be gold on a nearby island, he led an expedition to what is now Puerto Rico. De Leon found only a small amount of gold, but he started the first Spanish settlement there in 1508. The next year King Ferdinand of Spain named him governor of the island. Soon the king sent de Leon to explore lands to the north of Puerto Rico. De Leon set off in 1513 and landed in what is now Florida. He probably gave the region its name, which means "full of flowers" or "flowery."

conquistador—a leader in the Spanish conquest of North and South America during the 1500s

DE LEON IN FLORIDA

Ponce de Leon was the first Spaniard to have his government's permission to explore lands north of Puerto Rico, but he was not the first to land in Florida. Sometime before 1513, a slave trader named Diego de Miruelo landed in Florida during a storm.

De Leon came ashore near modern-day St. Augustine, Florida, but was quickly driven away by the local American Indian tribes, which included the Ais and Calusa. He eventually returned to Puerto Rico before going to Spain. King Ferdinand gave him permission to return to Florida as its governor. De Leon did not make the trip until 1521, and it ended badly. Once again he and his men battled the Calusa, who resisted the invasion of their lands. De Leon was wounded and his men took him to Cuba, where he died of his injuries.

Today Ponce de Leon might be best known for his supposed search for a fountain of youth. A Spanish historian said the Carib of Puerto Rico had told him about a magical fountain. Anyone who drank from the fountain would not grow old. The historian was friendly with the family of Christopher Columbus. They hated de Leon because they thought he wanted New World riches that belonged to them. So, the historian disliked him too. He wanted to make Ponce de Leon look foolish, so he made up the tale of the fountain of youth years after de Leon died.

NAMING A CONTINENT

By the time Ponce de Leon reached Florida, one of the continents of the New World had been called America. The name came from the Italian explorer Amerigo Vespucci. On voyages each year from 1499 to 1504, Vespucci explored the east coast of South America. During one of the trips, he realized that the lands he and Columbus were exploring were not part of Asia. Instead they were part of a "new world" Europeans had not known about before. In 1507 German mapmaker Martin Waldseemüller drew a world map that included the new continent Vespucci and others had explored. It was the first map to show the Atlantic and Pacific as separate oceans. On his map Waldseemüller called the new southern continent *America* in honor of the Italian adventurer. When another continent was mapped north of that region, it received the name America too—North America.

De Leon was believed to have searched for the fountain of youth on the island of Bimini.

-CHAPTER THREE-

Cartier Goes to Canada

While Spain and Portugal claimed parts of South America and Central America, other European leaders were looking to North America. During the 16th and 17th centuries, France was one of several countries that explored what became Canada. Sailing for France, Jacques Cartier led several expeditions to the Gulf of St. Lawrence and beyond.

Cartier aboard a ship arriving in Canada in the 1500s

Cartier was born in 1491 in the French coastal town of St. Malo. Before his Canada expeditions, he probably sailed on ships that explored Brazil and Newfoundland. European ships fished for cod off Newfoundland soon after Columbus reached the New World. King Francis of France sent Cartier to find a northern sea route to India and to search for gold in 1534.

THREE VOYAGES

Cartier sailed from France with two ships and reached Newfoundland in 20 days. He explored the west coast of Newfoundland before sailing around the Gulf of St. Lawrence. On the trip, he met some Iroquois Indians and swapped goods with them. It was the first recorded trade between the French and American Indians. Cartier also claimed some of the land he found for France.

-DISCOVERY FACT-

In 1524 Jacques Cartier may have sailed with Giovanni da Verrazzano, an Italian captain who worked for France. During that trip Verrazzano and his crew came ashore three times, in what is now North Carolina, New York City, and Rhode Island.

The next year Cartier sailed from France back up the St. Lawrence River and reached an Indian village that later became the city of Quebec. Cartier referred to the region around this spot as Canada. The name came from the Huron-Iroquois word *kanata,* which means "village." From there, Cartier sailed on to the spot that became the city of Montreal. An early winter that year trapped Cartier's ships in ice. About 25 men—a quarter of his crew—died from the cold or from disease. Finally, in the spring of 1536, the explorer and his crew returned to France.

Cartier made one last trip to Canada in 1541. He had not found gold or a sea route to India, but the American Indians told him he might find them farther west. King Francis also wanted to start a colony in the New World. Cartier sailed with five ships and about 1,500 people. Another group of colonists sailed after him. While exploring, Cartier thought he had found gold and diamonds. In the spring he sailed for France. Cartier was disappointed to learn that all he had found were worthless minerals. Cartier gave up exploring and remained in France until his death in 1557.

The other colonists stayed in Canada only a year. France would not try to start another colony there for more than 50 years. In 1603 Samuel de Champlain followed Cartier's route to Montreal. Champlain returned a few years later to start a permanent colony near the city of Quebec.

-CHAPTER FOUR-

Coronado's Quest for Gold

The desire for gold and other riches led to many of the European explorations of the New World. Unlike other explorers, however, Francisco de Coronado searched entirely on land. He and his men did not find gold, but they became the first Europeans to explore portions of what was to be become the heartland of the United States.

Francisco Vazquez de Coronado was born in Salamanca, Spain, around 1510. In 1535 he arrived in the Spanish colony of Mexico, which was known as New Spain. In 1538 the **viceroy** of the colony named Coronado the governor of Nueva Galicia, a region in the colony. Two years later Coronado teamed up with a Spanish priest named Marcos de Niza to explore what the Spaniards called Tierra Nueva, or "New Land." The region is now the southwestern part of the United States. De Niza had traveled through the region in 1539 and returned to Mexico with stories of the seven cities of Cibola, said to be filled with riches. He had not seen them himself, but de Niza was convinced they were real. The viceroy and Coronado used their own money to pay for a trip to find the seven cities of Cibola.

viceroy—a governor

Coronado erects a cross near the Missouri River.

ESTEBAN'S TRAVELS

Marcos de Niza had traveled north in 1538 with a former Moorish slave named Esteban. He had been part of a Spanish expedition sent to settle Florida in 1527. Rough seas destroyed several of the ships, and some colonists decided not to complete the voyage. Esteban was one of four men who came ashore in Florida and spent several years traveling with American Indians, including the Karankawa, before finally reaching Mexico.

Because of his travels, Esteban served as de Niza's messenger and guide on his trip northward. Esteban went ahead of the priest and sent back messages of the great wealth he found in Tierra Nueva. Esteban, though, angered the leaders of the **pueblo**, or village, thought to be one of the seven cities of Cibola. They killed him and some of the American Indians traveling with him. When a messenger told Marcos what happened, he returned to Mexico. Marcos was convinced that Cibola and the other nearby pueblos contained riches.

pueblo—the Spanish word for village, usually consisting of stone and adobe buildings; also, an American Indian tribe of New Mexico and Arizona that lived in pueblos

Coronado (on white horse) travels from Mexico through the American Southwest.

A LONG SEARCH FOR RICHES

In 1540 Coronado left Mexico, leading more than 1,300 men. More than half of them were Tlaxcalan, Tarascan, and Aztec Indians of Mexico who were friendly with the Spanish. That summer they reached what de Niza called Cibola. The native Zuni people called the pueblo Hawikuh. Coronado's men saw a large mud-brick building. They attacked it and killed hundreds of Zunis. But they did not find gold and other valuables. Coronado said that de Niza "has not spoken the truth in anything he said."

Still desperate to find gold, Coronado and his men pushed on. They came to more pueblos and stole food. Coronado often treated the native peoples brutally. Some Pueblo Indians fled as the Spaniards came to their villages. Coronado then heard tales of a wealthy place to the north called Quivira. He left with some of his men to find it. To get to Quivira, the expedition traveled through parts of what are now Texas, Oklahoma, and Kansas. When Coronado reached Quivira, he realized he had been tricked. The city did not have great riches. The Spanish then began their long march back to Mexico. Coronado remained in government service in Mexico until his death in 1554.

Although Coronado did not find gold, he traveled farther into the interior of North America than any European before him. He saw large herds of buffalo on the Great Plains and crossed the **Continental Divide**. Some of his men went on a side expedition and became the first Europeans to see the Grand Canyon. He also met a wide range of native peoples, from the pueblo dwellers who spoke several different languages to the Wichita of the plains.

Continental Divide—the stretch of high ground formed by the crests of the Rocky Mountains. Rivers on the east flow to the Atlantic Ocean and rivers on the west flow to the Pacific Ocean

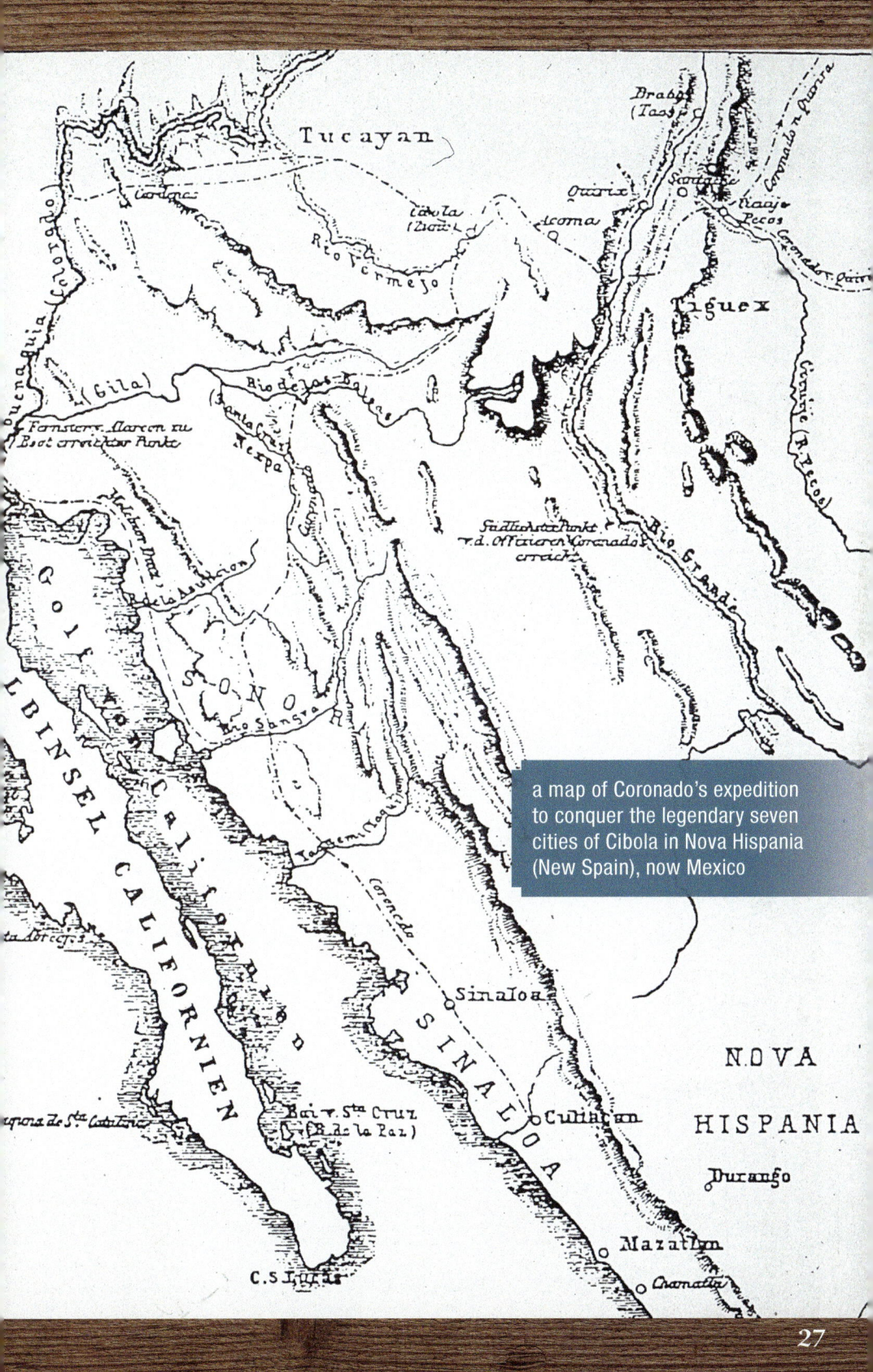

a map of Coronado's expedition to conquer the legendary seven cities of Cibola in Nova Hispania (New Spain), now Mexico

-CHAPTER FIVE-

Drake Circles the World

As Spain built up its New World colonies, it often came into conflict with England. England's Queen Elizabeth I sent Francis Drake on a secret mission in 1577. He and his men were to attack Spanish ships and ports along the Pacific Coast of the Americas. On that mission Drake also explored the coast along present-day California.

AN EARLY LIFE AT SEA

Drake was born in Tavistock, England, around 1541. In his early teens, he served as an **apprentice** on a small ship. By the 1560s Drake was sailing with his second cousin John Hawkins. Hawkins captained English ships that carried slaves to the Americas. The voyages Hawkins and Drake made were dangerous because Spanish ships attacked them. To the Spanish, Drake was a pirate. Spanish hatred of Drake increased during the 1570s because he captured several Spanish ships filled with silver. Drake kept some of the silver and gave the rest to his queen.

> **apprentice**—someone who learns a trade by working with a skilled person

Francis Drake

Queen Elizabeth knights Francis Drake.

A LONG VOYAGE

On his secret mission in 1577, Drake set off with five ships. Only his ship the *Golden Hind* was able to complete the voyage. Drake and his crew sailed through a strait near the southern tip of South America before heading north. Along the way they attacked Spanish ports and captured Spanish ships. Drake hoped to find a sea route back to the Atlantic Ocean. He sailed perhaps as far as present-day Washington state but never found the route he was searching for because it didn't exist. No other European explorer had traveled this far north along North America's Pacific Coast.

Drake turned back south, and in June 1579, he came ashore near what is now San Francisco, California. He claimed the land for England and called it *Nova Albion*—Latin for "New England." After repairing his ship and trading gifts with local natives, Drake headed west across the Pacific Ocean. He and his crew reached England in 1580. The *Golden Hind* was just the second ship to **circumnavigate** the globe. To honor him, Queen Elizabeth made Drake a knight, which gave him the title "sir."

circumnavigate—to sail or travel completely around the world

31

Drake's sailing career was far from over. During the 1580s he kept attacking Spanish ships and ports. In one attack he and his crew destroyed more than 30 Spanish ships. He was still sailing in 1596. But off the coast of Panama, he developed a disease that killed him. His crew buried him at sea.

Drake proved his skills as both a navigator and a fighter. His circumnavigation helped increase Europe's understanding of world geography. And his visit to California made an impact too. Although England did not start a colony there, Drake's explorations fueled interest in starting other American colonies.

—DISCOVERY FACT—

Thanks to his raids on Spanish ships and ports, Sir Francis Drake captured silver and other valuables worth millions of dollars in today's money. Queen Elizabeth used her share of the wealth to pay debts she owed to foreign countries.

The British and Spanish battle in British waters in 1588.

-CHAPTER SIX-

Hudson Reaches New York

By the early 1600s, the Netherlands entered the race to find riches in Asia. Dutch traders were interested in finding a northerly and western route to Asia. Henry Hudson, an English sea captain, believed he could find that route by sailing far north of where Columbus had sailed. Hudson turned to the Dutch East India Company to finance the trip and set off in 1609. Hudson never reached Asia, but he paved the way for the Netherlands to start its first colony in the New World.

SAILING NORTH

Little is known about Hudson's early life, except that he was born in England around 1565. By 1607 he was working for the Muscovy Company, an English trading company seeking a northern route to Asia. They paid for Hudson to make two voyages. He sailed north on the first trip and then northeast on the second to try to reach Asia.

Hudson and his crew had to turn back each time because ice blocked their path. In 1608 when Muscovy said no to a third trip, the Dutch approached Hudson. With their backing, Hudson and his crew sailed to the New World in April 1609.

Henry Hudson

Hudson drew on the work of previous explorers who suggested two paths to follow. One path would go north in Canada. The other was farther to the south. Explorer John Smith had suggested that a sea route cut across North America starting around Virginia. Hudson chose that route.

After reaching Newfoundland, Hudson sailed his ship the *Half Moon* south along the eastern coast of North America. Hudson took the ship as far as present-day North Carolina before turning north again.

cultivation—the raising of crops

Hudson's map of his voyages in the Arctic

Hudson looked for a river that could be the route Smith had talked about. In the process, Hudson and his crew became the first Europeans to reach present-day Delaware Bay. But the waters there were dangerous, so they sailed on.

Soon the ship reached what is now New York Harbor. Hudson sailed up the widest river that emptied into the harbor. Along the way Hudson and some of his men went ashore. Hudson wrote that the land "is the finest for **cultivation** that I ever in my life set foot upon."

-DISCOVERY FACT-

John Smith was one of the expedition leaders who started the English colony of Jamestown, Virginia, in 1607. As an explorer he sailed along the coasts of modern-day Maine and Massachusetts and gave the region its name — New England.

Hudson and his men met American Indians both around New York Harbor and during their voyage up the large river. Most were friendly but at times they clashed with the Europeans. Hudson saw that the American Indians trapped and traded furs. His exploration ended when the river became too shallow for his ship to sail. He then returned to Europe.

Hudson stopped in England, perhaps to drop off some English sailors who had made the trip. The English would not let him sail to the Netherlands, since he was aiding a foreign rival. But Hudson was able to send a report, the ship's official record, and his notes to the Netherlands. The Dutch East India Company decided to begin trading for furs with the American Indians of what is now New York. Later, the river Hudson found was named for him.

But Hudson never sailed the river again. He wanted to try once more to find a northwest route to Asia. This time wealthy Englishmen were ready to back him. Hudson sailed on the *Discovery* in 1610 and reached a bay in Canada, which would later also be named for him. After spending the winter trapped in ice, most of Hudson's crew turned against him. They forced the captain, his son, and several others to enter a small boat and set it adrift. They were never heard from again.

Hudson meets with American Indians along the Hudson River.

Hudson never found the Northwest Passage he sought, but he helped two European countries expand their empires. The Dutch started the colony of New Amsterdam at the mouth of the Hudson River. It later became New York. England claimed the land around Hudson Bay.

-CHAPTER SEVEN-

Joliet and Marquette Go Down the Mississippi

After starting its colony near the city of Quebec, France sought to extend its influence over Canada. It focused on the area around the St. Lawrence River and the Great Lakes. By the 1660s French fur traders were working along the western banks of Lake Superior. In 1672 France chose Louis Joliet and Jacques Marquette to explore the lands south of the Great Lakes and look for the river the Indians called Messipi, or "Great Water."

THE TRADER AND THE MISSIONARY

Joliet was a fur trader and mapmaker born around 1645 near Quebec. Marquette was born in 1637 in Laon, France. He was a Roman Catholic **missionary** who came to Canada to convert the American Indians to his faith. He quickly learned several dialects of the Algonquin language. Together these two and five other men set off in canoes from what is now called Lake Michigan. They followed several smaller rivers south before reaching the waterway now known as the Mississippi River. During this and other parts of the trip, the men sometimes had to carry their canoes from one body of water to another.

As a priest, Marquette wore a long, dark robe. Some American Indians they met recognized the robes and realized the explorers had not come to attack. The chief of the Peoria Indians gave Marquette a peace pipe called a **calumet**. The pipe came in handy when the explorers later met the Quapaw Indians, who seemed ready to attack them. As Marquette held up the pipe, the Quapaw realized the intruders were friendly.

missionary—a person who does religious or charitable work in a territory or foreign country

calumet—a Native American pipe that was recognized as a sign of peace

Though they didn't speak the same language, the French explorers and American Indians communicated in other ways. Symbols such as a calumet meant the explorers came in peace.

From the Quapaw, Marquette and Joliet learned that other Europeans lived farther down the river. The Frenchmen realized that the American Indians were describing Spanish settlers and soldiers who lived near what is now called the Gulf of Mexico. Marquette and Joliet figured that the Mississippi River entered that gulf. They did not want to come into a possible conflict with the Spaniards, so they began to make their way back up the river.

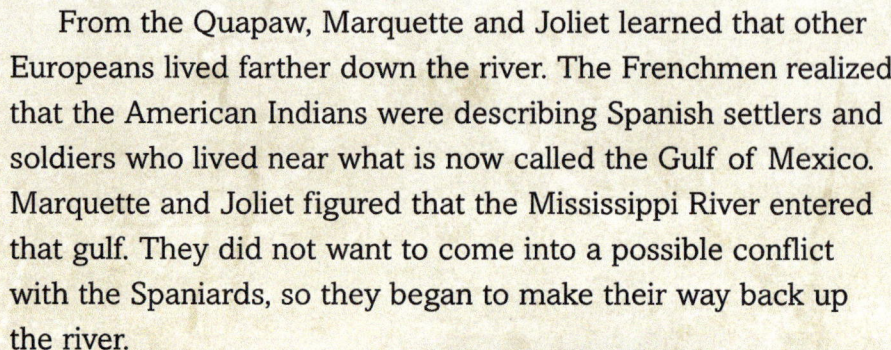

-DISCOVERY FACT-

The Peoria Indian chief whom Marquette and Joliet met trusted them enough to send his 10-year-old son with them as a guide. The boy showed the explorers a shortcut to take when they made their return trip up the Mississippi River.

The expedition took a different route back to Lake Michigan, along the Illinois and Chicago rivers. The region had prairie land filled with tall grass. Joliet saw that building a canal from the Illinois River to Lake Michigan would give France control over the trade in the area. They could easily travel from the Great Lakes down the Mississippi River.

Marquette and Joliet were the first white men on the upper Mississippi.

When the trip was over, Marquette stayed in the region to convert more natives to Christianity. He became ill in 1675 and died. Joliet headed back to Quebec to tell officials there what he had learned. The voyage turned deadly in the St. Lawrence River. Rough waters flipped over Joliet's canoe, killing three people. Joliet clung to rocks for several hours before he was rescued. He lost all of his notes in the accident. He had to rely on his memory to report all that he had learned. Luckily, most of the notes Marquette took were preserved because he was not on the voyage.

Joliet hoped to return to the area around the Chicago River and start a colony. France, though, was not interested in that. The area later became the site of the city of Chicago. The Joliet and Marquette expedition did not lead to new settlements. But the expedition gave Europeans new knowledge about the geography of North America.

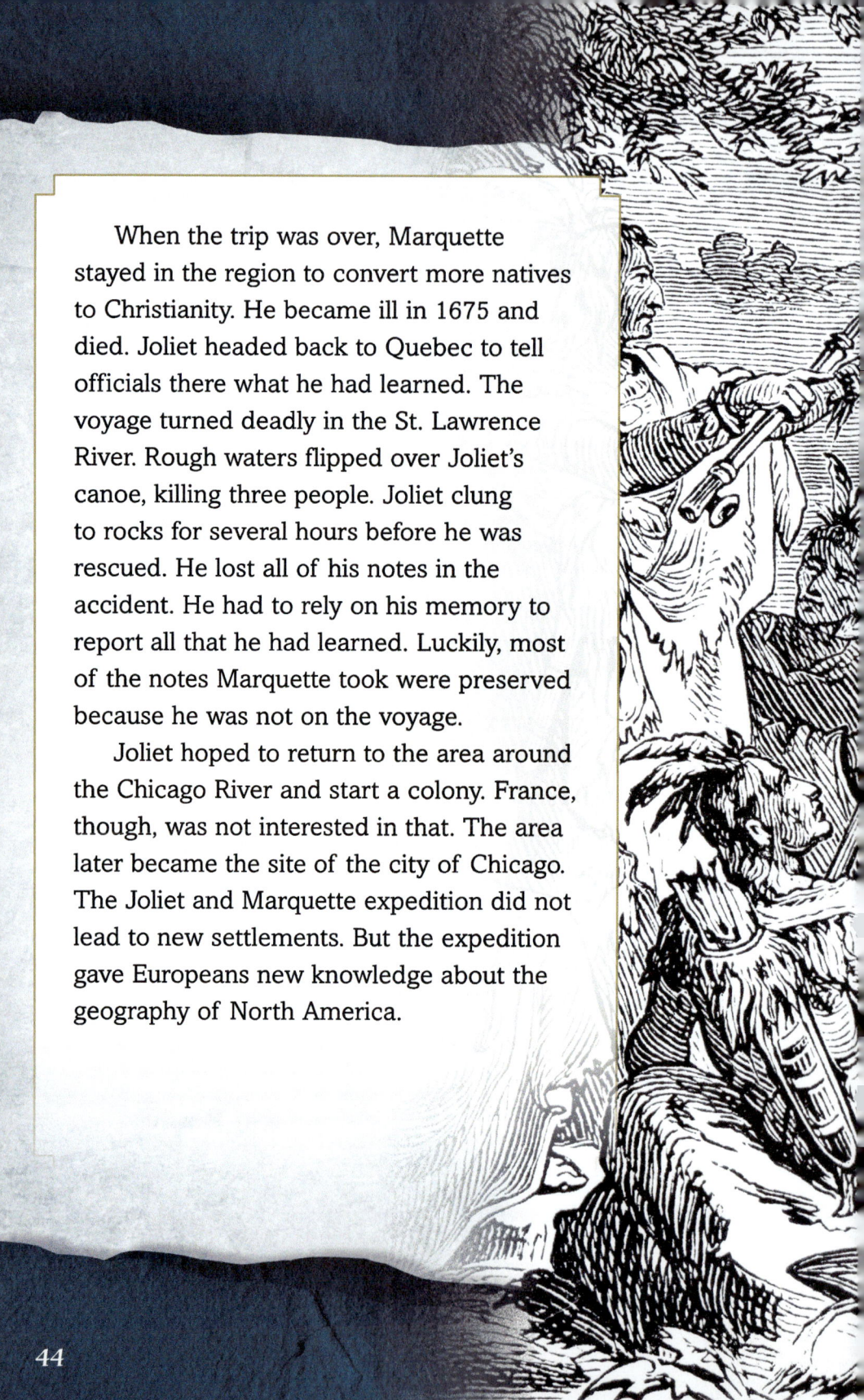

Marquette's main mission was to teach American Indians about Christianity.

Glossary

apprentice (uh-PREN-tiss)—someone who learns a trade by working with a skilled person

calumet (KAL-yuh-met)—a Native American pipe that was recognized as a sign of peace

circumnavigate (suhr-kuhm-NAV-uh-gayt)—to sail or travel completely around the world

conquistador (kon-KEYS-tuh-dor)—a leader in the Spanish conquest of North and South America during the 1500s

Continental Divide (kahn-tuh-NEN-tuhl duh-VYD)—the stretch of high ground formed by the crests of the Rocky Mountains. Rivers on the east flow to the Atlantic Ocean and rivers on the west flow to the Pacific Ocean

convert (kuhn-VURT)—to change religion

cultivation (kuhl-uh-VAY-shuhn)—the raising of crops

expedition (ek-spuh-DI-shuhn)—a journey made for a particular reason

missionary (MISH-uh-nayr-ee)—a person who does religious or charitable work in a territory or foreign country

pueblo (PWEB-loh)—the Spanish word for village, usually consisting of stone and adobe buildings; also, an American Indian tribe of New Mexico and Arizona that lived in pueblos

viceroy (VYE-sur-oy)—a governor

Read More

Cooke, Tim. *The Exploration of North America*. Explorers Discovering the World. New York: Gareth Stevens, 2013.

Gunderson, Jessica. *Conquistadors: Fearsome Fighters*. Fearsome Fighters. Mankato, Minn.: Creative Education, 2013.

Higgins, Nadia. *Columbus and the Journey to the New World*. History of America. Vero Beach, Fla.: Rourke Educational Media, 2013

Critical Thinking Using the Common Core

1. Why did the countries of Europe explore and then try to start colonies in the New World? (Key Ideas and Details)

2. If you had to pick one of the explorers to travel with, which would it be, and why? (Integration of Knowledge and Ideas)

3. After Columbus, which explorer made the most trips to the New World? (Key Ideas and Details)

Internet Sites

FactHound offers a safe, fun way to find Internet sites related to this book. All of the sites on FactHound have been researched by our staff.

Here's all you do:
Visit *www.facthound.com*
Type in this code: 9781515718680

Index

Africa, *5, 6, 11, 12*
Ais, *15*
Algonquin, *40*
Arawak, *10*
Asia, *4, 5, 6, 9, 11, 16, 34, 38*
Atlantic Ocean, *8, 16, 31*
Aztec, *25*

California, *28, 31, 32*
Calusa, *15*
Canada, *18, 19, 20, 21, 36, 38, 40*
Carib, *12, 16*
Caribbean Sea, *5, 10, 12*
Cartier, Jacques, *18, 19, 20*
Central America, *10, 18*
Cibola, *22, 24*
Columbian Exchange, *11*
Columbus, Christopher, *4, 5, 6, 8, 9, 10, 11, 12, 16, 19, 34*
Cuba, *10, 15*

de Champlain, Samuel, *21*
de Coronado, Francisco, *22, 25, 26*
de Leon, Juan Ponce, *12, 14, 15, 16*
de Miruelo, Diego, *15*
de Niza, Marcos, *22, 24, 25*
Drake, Francis, *28, 31, 32*
Dutch East India Company, *34, 38*

England, *28, 32, 34, 38*

Florida, *14, 15, 16, 24*
France, *18, 19, 20, 21, 40, 43, 44*

Great Lakes, *40, 43*
Gulf of St. Lawrence, *18, 19*

Hawkins, John, *28*
Hispaniola, *10, 12*
Hudson, Henry, *34, 36, 37, 38, 39*
Huron, *20*

India, *19, 20*
Iroquois, *19, 20*

Joliet, Louis, *40, 42, 43, 44*

Karankawa, *24*
King Ferdinand, *5, 14, 15*
King Francis, *19, 20*

Marquette, Jacques, *40, 41, 42, 44*
Mexico, *22, 24, 25, 26*
Mississippi River, *40, 42, 43*
Montreal, *20, 21*
Muscovy Company, *34*

Netherlands, *34, 38*
Newfoundland, *19, 36*
North America, *16, 18, 26, 31, 36, 44*

Pacific Ocean, *16, 31*
Peoria, *41, 42*
Portugal, *6, 18*
Pueblo, *26*
Puerto Rico, *14, 15, 16*

Quapaw, *41, 42*
Quebec, *20, 21, 40, 44*
Queen Elizabeth I, *28, 31*
Queen Isabella, *5*

Smith, John, *36, 37*
South America, *10, 16, 18, 31*
Spain, *4, 5, 6, 9, 10, 12, 14, 15, 18, 22, 28*
St. Lawrence River, *20, 40, 44*

Taino, *10*
Tarascan, *25*
Tlaxcalan, *25*

Vespucci, Amerigo, *16*
Virginia, *36, 37*

Waldseemüller, Martin, *16*
Wichita, *26*

Zuni, *25*